How to Be Your Little Man's Dad

365 THINGS TO DO WITH YOUR SON

DAN BOLIN AND KEN SUTTERFIELD

OUR GUARANTEE TO YOU

We believe so strongly in the message of our books that we are making this quality guarantee to you. If for any reason you are disappointed with the content of this book, return the title page to us with your name and address and we will refund to you the list price of the book. To help us serve you better, please briefly describe why you were disappointed. Mail your refund request to: PiñonPress, P.O. Box 35002, Colorado Springs, CO 80935.

Library of Congress Catalog Card Number:
93-85141

ISBN 08910-97554

Printed in the United States of America

9 10 11 12 13 14 15 16 / 08 07 06 05 04 03

To Real Dads

❖

Warren Bolin and Keith Sutterfield

INTRODUCTION

❖

Boys need real dads. Not just fathers to put food on the table, set curfews, and make sons clean the garage, they need real dads. Real dads play catch, lead hikes in the woods, tell stories at bedtime, and wrestle on the living room carpet.

I (Dan) grew up with a real dad. He didn't catch many fish—he was too busy baiting hooks for my brothers and me. He pitched baseballs at Columbia Park until we were tired of swinging the bat. He carried the heavy pack so we could hike together to remote lakes in the Cascade and Olympic Mountains.

Real dads shoot their sons like arrows to impact the next generation. It is tough to be a real dad. The price to become one must be paid in time and commitment. Our world is short of both; there are demands and distractions that call us away from the things that matter most.

When our family goes out for pizza I find myself drawn to the game "Gopher Heads." I love to stand with mallet in hand, slip my token into the machine, and await the battle. A gopher head appears, I strike with precision, and it disappears into its hole. Two heads appear at once. Like lightning I nail one, then the other. The battle has been joined. Heads appear faster and faster, more and more of them. I frantically strike, strike, and strike. Some escape my blows, but most are defeated. At the peak of the warfare the light goes off, the music ends, and the gopher heads retreat to their dens. They will lick their wounds and await my next token.

"Gopher Heads" fill my days. Appointments, phone calls, meetings, questions, and problems come at me relentlessly. I defeat one and face two more. I want normalcy, rest, and quiet, but at the same time, I love the adrenaline rush of fighting "Gopher Heads."

The losers in this battle are the dads who don't know when or how to call a truce. We love the smell of the battle, so we fight late into the evening, spend Saturdays in the office getting caught up, and often bring the battle home with us.

The other losers, of course, are our wives, daughters, and sons.

Sons lose the security of knowing they are worth more to us than a corner office. They lose the instruction that can be given only when they are ready to ask the question. They lose the mentoring of a tested warrior.

After writing *How to Be Your Daughter's Daddy*, I was asked to write this companion, *How to Be Your Little Man's Dad*. I could write with the credibility of a grateful son, but my personal experience was as the father of daughters. I needed some help, and I knew where to find it.

Ken Sutterfield's sons, Ragan and Spencer, were 3 and 2 when Ken and his wife, Jan, came to work for Pine Cove. At the time, my daughter Catie was 2, and Haley had not yet arrived on the scene. Our young families were intertwined with the strong bonds of friendship. This allowed me to watch Ken and Jan do the things that grow little boys into men.

They are artists, blending the colors of love and discipline along with the hues of creativity and consistency to paint portraits of wonderful young men. Not perfect parents, not perfect parenting, but making each stroke of the brush count to give their sons the character and competency they will need to face adulthood.

Life is a never-ending series of changes and dads must listen to the call of opportunity. They must test their skills against greater challenges, but they must test their hearts against the worth of their sons. Greater challenges and leadership took Ken and his family from directing the adult and family operations at Pine Cove in Tyler, Texas, to the executive directorship of Ozark Conference Center near Little Rock, Arkansas.

A father's life can be filled with building bigger barns to store our achievements and wealth. We are eager to respond to the deep desire to achieve and accomplish. In the process of building bigger barns, fathers must be very careful not to destroy the priceless little barns. The valuable little barns in many men's lives are their sons. Too often the price that is paid on the way to the top is the souls of the sons.

Ken built a bigger barn, but he was careful not to dismantle the little barns in his life.

Our families remain very close. My wife, Cay, and I have had the privilege of viewing the Sutterfield boys growth over several months instead of in daily increments. They aren't yet grown, and there are no guarantees that their paths will be free of trauma. But Ken and Jan have worked the odds in favor of their sons through love and sacrifice.

Ken is a great dad. He acquired his skill from another great dad. Keith Sutterfield was busy in the newspaper business while Ken was growing up, yet he found the time to instill the essential qualities of life into the character of his son.

I had the privilege of reading a letter Keith sent to Ken shortly after Catie, then nine years old, lost her battle with leukemia. Keith was still dad, sharing wisdom, encouraging, and instructing Ken to be a strong friend to our family in the cold, dark valley of our child's death.

We recently visited Ken, Jan, Ragan, and Spencer, staying in their home. Skeletons of birds, cages with snakes, collections of rocks, and posters of athletes fill the boys' rooms. Pictures of family and friends, books of adventure and information, music, and conversation fill their home.

Ken is busy, but not too busy for his sons.

That's why I was compelled to ask Ken to work with me on this book. I've learned a lot as we have shared ideas and remembered wonderful moments. I've been reminded of events and projects that the routine and pressures of life had pushed to the back corners of my mind.

As we have worked together I have realized that life is a series of wonderful, curious, powerful, eternal moments that form the collections we call "life." These collections of moments change little boys into men. Moments can be cold, hurtful, painful, destructive, or meaningless, scattered in disarray over the days of childhood. Or they can be warm, strong, joyful, healthy, and intentional, ordered to create insightful, stable, noble young men who are able to meet the challenges of the next generation and beyond.

Dads must be involved in these moments of maturation. They must invest time, energy, and wisdom to make each moment achieve its strategic impact.

Since our societies have moved from the country to the big city and from the farm to the office, many dads have lost touch with the hearts of their children. The core of many father's worth and satisfaction exists at the work place. Home becomes an annoyance, a sideshow, or a disposable appendage. Dads have learned to delegate tasks. Making good decisions is the greatest skill to be acquired in the information age. After a long day of decision making the easiest decision is to delegate the child-rearing to Mom. Children need Mom, but they need Dad too.

Sons need the model of maleness that they can best find in their father. They need Mom's love and warmth, but they need Dad's love and strength.

It seems odd to me that when a mom spends time with her children she is "parenting." But when it is a dad's turn to watch the children we say he is "baby-sitting." The difference between parenting and baby-sitting has to do with the motivation of the heart and the length of the impact. Dads need to parent with a heart of love and with a desire to prepare each son (or daughter) for a life that will make a difference for generations to come.

No father's deathbed regret is that he did not spend enough time at work and too much time with his son. The pain of misplaced priorities has haunted many "successful" fathers. We don't intentionally destroy the souls of our sons, we just fail to attend to their needs. The natural course of events, free from a father's support and guidance, claims its prey.

But somehow our kids "make it." Somehow, despite our carelessness, ignorance, and incompetence as fathers, our kids make it. The challenge is to help them make it with as much strength, skill, wisdom, and confidence as possible.

Ken and I desire that we be real dads—that we make a positive impact on our children. We hope that this book will help you become the best dad your little man could ever hope for.

1

Tell him his muscles look bigger.

❖

2

Show him the proper use of your pocketknife.

❖

3

When he is ready,
give him your pocketknife.

4
Ask him his opinion
on things that are important to you.

❖

5
Say "yes" as much as possible.

❖

6
Teach him to call 911.

7
Don't make promises
you are not willing to keep.

❖

8
Don't make threats you are not willing to enforce.

❖

9
Talk openly about current events.
Engage him in the conversation.

10

Give him access to lumber, hammer, and nails,
and let him create.

❖

11

Show him how to spin a basketball
on his finger.

❖

12

Keep his picture at work.

13

Teach him how to mow the yard,
and work with him.

❖

14

Give him the opportunity
to go with you
to meet important people.

15

Write about him to grandparents
and friends.
Show him what you have written.

❖

16

Tell him stories about yourself
when you were his age.

17
Give him your business card,
and tell him he can call you anytime.

❖

18
Take him with you on a short business trip.

❖

19
Bring a glass of water to him at bedtime
before he asks.

20
Admit you are wrong and apologize.

❖

21
Know the names of his friends
and as much as you can about them.

❖

22
Volunteer to visit his class
and tell the students about your profession.

23
Work together to wash the car
and then his bike.

❖

24
Go fishing with him.

❖

25
Clean and cook his fish
no matter how small.

26
Invite him to drink hot chocolate with you
while you enjoy
your morning coffee.

27
Go sledding with him
on a cookie sheet.

28

Plant a tree together,
and watch it grow.

29

Take him to your childhood home
and show him the old neighborhood.

30
Give him the last piece of dessert.

31
Have a water-balloon fight and get wet.

32
Look at the picture album of his first few years,
and tell him stories.

33
Let him have unusual pets—tarantula, snake, domestic rat, etc.

❖

34
Give him your childhood coin collection.

❖

35
Take your son to an orchard or berry farm to pick fresh fruit.

36

Camp out in your living room (tent and all).

37

Let him stay up late to watch
an old western movie with you.

38

Turn up the radio in the car,
and roll down the windows.

39

Teach him to shake hands firmly
and look a man in the eye.

40

Be a student of your son.
Know his strengths, abilities,
and weaknesses.

41

When you will be away overnight,
leave him a sack with a surprise
for each day you will be gone.

❖

42

Teach him how to make a football spiral.

❖

43

Live a life of integrity.

44

Have a drawer or box in your office
where he can keep things.

❖

45

Have a sock war—
five minutes and twenty pairs of socks.

❖

46

Ride scary rides together at the fair.

47
Open the hood of your car
and show him the parts of the engine.

❖

48
Lay out under the stars together.

❖

49
Keep holidays and birthdays special.

50

Walk through an unfinished house
with your son.

51

Build a treehouse together.

52

Teach him how to ride
the city bus or subway.

53
Go on a two-man campout.

54
Take him on a surprise adventure
to the country after school.

55
Help him identify poisonous plants
near your home.

56
Together, assemble a model airplane.

57
Write your son a letter
telling him the things he does well
and the positive character traits you see in him.

58
Read him stories of great national heroes.

59
Send him a telegram when you cannot be there
for a special event in his life.

❖

60
Give him your old billfold.
"Accidentally" leave a dollar hidden in it.

❖

61
Cut off an old belt of yours to fit him.

62

Speak highly of the women in your life.
Help him learn to value
their character and skill.

❖

63

Play together in the mud.

❖

64

Teach him to play checkers and to play chess.

65

Give him a box of disguises.
Fill it with old hats, coats,
glasses, wigs, etc.

66

Teach him to tie his own tie.

67

Take him to a hands-on museum.

68

Let him ride the coin-operated pony
outside the grocery store
after he has cooperated inside the store.

❖

69

Take him to visit
a woodworking or cabinet shop.

70
Help him make figures out of clay.

71
Give him a kit
with his own shoe polishing equipment.
Teach him to polish his own shoes.

72
Pay him to polish your shoes.

73
Let him ride and ride the escalator loop
while the family is shopping.

❖

74
Give him pennies to throw
in the mall fountain if he has cooperated
while you were shopping.

75
Take him to ride a go-cart.

❖

76
Require him to send his own thank-you notes.

❖

77
Make sure he knows where you keep
a hidden house key.

78
Give him sidewalk chalk and let him create.

❖

79
Teach him to blow a bubble with bubble gum.

❖

80
Let him teach you something
from his area of expertise.

81
Teach him sports lingo.

❖

82
Teach him sports protocol.

❖

83
Make sure his name is clearly marked
on his baseball glove.

84
Encourage him to take guitar lessons.

85
Give him the equipment he will need
for a campout.

86
Read him books about inventors.

87

Let him wear your boots,
even though they are too big.

88

Walk together in the woods.
Let him take the lead.

89
Teach him table manners.

90
Hug and love his mother.

91
Plant and care for a garden together.

92
Create a special hand signal
that only you and your son
will understand.

93
Let him help you with a project,
even if it will take a little longer.

94
Hold the jar
while he puts the big spider in it.

❖

95
Take him on a paddle boat ride.

❖

96
Teach him to whittle safely.

97
Take him to breakfast—his choice.

❖

98
Let him paint the deck or driveway
with water.

❖

99
Give him his own special treasure chest (box)
so he can store his most valued possessions.

100
Enjoy a fresh coconut together.

❖

101
Give him every opportunity
to participate in at least one team sport.

❖

102
Take him to a shop
that produces handmade toys.

103

Display a clay handprint
of his five-year-old hand
at home or in your office.

104

Give him the equipment
he will need
to participate in various sports.

105
Let him get dirty. It washes off.

❖

106
Give him his own pocket change
to share with the Salvation Army bell ringers
during the Christmas season.

107
Make a batch of chocolate chip cookies together,
but don't bake them—
just eat the dough.
Freeze what is left over to bake another time.

❖

108
Teach him how to fold the American flag.

109
Stop to watch the activity
at a construction site together.

❖

110
Teach him the names and functions
of the machinery and equipment
at the construction site.

111
Work a jigsaw puzzle with your son.

❖

112
Build and paint a birdhouse together.

❖

113
Designate a tree for the birds in your yard.
String popcorn and hang bird feeders.

114

Take him on a boat ride. Teach him
the meaning of "port" and "starboard."

❖

115

Count the number of seconds
between the time you see the lightning
and when you hear the thunder.

116
Take him with you
to kick tires on a used car lot.

117
Show him how to tie a few special knots.

118
Go to the airport together
to watch airplanes take off and land.

119
Help him climb a tree safely.

120
Arrange for a visit with a forest ranger.

121
Run together in a community fun run.

122
Teach him how to tap out his name
in Morse code.

❖

123
Create a treasure map for him to follow
to a special surprise.

124

Write a check to your son.
Take him to your bank
and let him choose
whether he wants to cash the check
or use it to start his own savings account.

❖

125

Get to know the parents of his friends.

126

Hike together to a mountaintop or overlook
where you can see for miles.

127

Rearrange the living room furniture
and have a world championship
wrestling match.

128
Teach him to handle a BB gun safely.

129
Never allow him to point a gun at anyone
(not even a toy or imaginary gun).

130
Do not interrupt him when he is talking.

131
Provide him with opportunities
that allow him to excel
in his areas of giftedness.

132
Ask him questions to keep him talking
and to show him
that you were really listening.

133

Look at him when he is talking.

❖

134

Call home and ask for him by name.

❖

135

Tuck him into bed.

136

Help him get started with a collection
he is interested in—coins, stamps,
baseball cards, whatever.

137

Honk the car horn
whenever you are in tunnels.

138
Choose a service project
you are both interested in
to work on with your son.

139
Enjoy snowcones together
on a hot summer day.

140
Rake leaves together.

141
Play in the leaves you have raked.

142
Build a fire and roast marshmallows.

143
Give him something your father gave you.

❖

144
Let him push the elevator buttons.

❖

145
Talk about things that go on and on forever
while looking at the stars.

146
Play catch.

❖

147
Attend all his special programs and events.

❖

148
Give him piggyback rides.

149
Teach him to swim.

150
Teach him to dive.

151
Know his favorite food and drink.

152
Lead special cheers for his mother.

153
On nights when Mom is gone, make it a party.

154
Put extra butter on the popcorn.

155
Order sea monkeys
and watch them grow.

❖

156
Go to his class and carve a pumpkin.

❖

157
Let him sit next to you in the car to steer
on a country road.

158
Show him how to skip a rock on water.

159
Help him learn various bird calls.

160
Build a snowman together.

161
Take him to a professional baseball game.
Get seats as close to the dugout as possible.

❖

162
Wash your hands before dinner,
and share a towel to dry them.

❖

163
Let him copy his hand on a photocopy machine.

164

Encourage him to help you when you paint.

❖

165

Let him be who he is and not who you are.

❖

166

Put a hummingbird feeder
outside his bedroom window.

167
Be available and willing
to taxi him to special events.

❖

168
Encourage his creative inventions.

❖

169
Explore a farm together.

170

Buy him a yo-yo,
and show him how to do some yo-yo tricks.

❖

171

Tell him about the lessons you took as a child
and what was good about them.

❖

172

Help him make his own video movie.

173
Encourage him to take his mom on a date.

174
Look at a picture album together,
and talk about family memories.

175
Take him on a visit to your local fire station.

176
Encourage him to talk about his hopes
and dreams for the future.

❖

177
Serve Mom breakfast in bed.

❖

178
Go shopping together for a gift for Mom.

179
Thank him for being your son,
no strings attached.

❖

180
Give him your old briefcase
and leave some official-looking papers
for him to play with.

181

Introduce him to men you respect.
Comment on their best qualities
so your son will learn
what to model his life after.

182

Go ice skating together.
Teach him the fine points of falling down.

183

Take him to a magic store.
Select a trick you can learn together.
Perform it, and any other tricks you know,
for the rest of the family.

❖

184

Go to a Christmas tree farm.
Let your son select the tree.

185
Let him record the message
on your telephone answering machine.

❖

186
Go on a hay ride together.

❖

187
Involve your son when you do a favorite hobby.

188
Teach him to "shave."
Give him a bladeless razor,
and show him how to lather up
and shave with you.

189
Give him an allowance
that is dependent on his completion
of assigned chores around the house.

190

Teach him how to put gas in the car.
Make sure he can surprise his mom
with this new skill
the next time you are together in the car.

191

Help him choose a summer camp
that has activities he is interested in
that will also help him grow.

192
Watch a sunrise together.

❖

193
Go to his school
and eat lunch with him
and anyone else he wants to include.

❖

194
Teach him a song, and sing it together.

195
Surprise him
with a magazine subscription all his own.
Make sure it is addressed
in his name.

196
When he loses a tooth,
celebrate a "Tooth-Out Day."

197
Teach him to ride a bicycle safely
with hand signals.

❖

198
Go bike riding—
just the two of you.

199
Help him catch a butterfly.
Help him mount the butterfly
you caught together.

200
Take him to visit a photo darkroom
and see how negatives
and prints are made.

201
Play a game of "HORSE" together.
You must shoot the basketball with the hand
you do not favor.
This should give your son the advantage.

❖

202
Give him the family junk mail to open.

203
Guard your tongue.
Harsh words can never be retrieved.

204
Take him horseback riding.

205
Take lots of pictures of him.

206
Visit a petting zoo
and discover the animals together.

❖

207
Make a pie or cake together.
It will taste great no matter how it turns out.

❖

208
Together, build a kite and fly it.

209
Start a rock collection.
Find an interesting rock each time
you have a family outing or vacation.

❖

210
Take him to a small circus.
Let him see the performers
and events up close.

211

Go to a leather craft shop.
Select a simple project
your son would like
to make together for him.

212

Give your son a disposable camera.
Let him take pictures at his discretion.

213
Build an obstacle course
in your back yard.
Take turns running through it.
(Be sure to time each other.)

214
Go to a T-shirt shop
and design identical shirts.
Wear them with pride.

215
Play Monopoly.
Leave the game set up for months,
if necessary.

216
Help him write letters
to his grandparents.

217

Build a doghouse and paint it
the colors and pattern of your dog.

218

Show him how to start a fire
with a magnifying glass.
Talk about the safety precautions
for doing this later on his own.

219
Help him catch a crawdad.

❖

220
Find a way to let him milk a cow.

❖

221
Catch a tadpole and let him keep it
until it develops into a frog.

222

Take him to the site of a military battle.
Explain to him that our freedom
cost a great many people a great price.

223

When visiting another city,
look in the phone book
to see if you can find someone
with the same name as your son.

224

When your city's symphony
gives a special performance for youth,
take him to see it.

❖

225

Save your pennies in a jar.
Give them to him
when there are enough for him
to roll and turn in for a couple dollars.

226
Help him with his homework,
but don't do it for him.

❖

227
Tell him about his great-grandparents.

❖

228
Give him a ride in a wheelbarrow.

229

Take time to review his school work
and other projects.

❖

230

Tell him you are excited
about the answers he got right,
and don't focus on the ones he got wrong.

231

As a family, go to see a live nativity scene during the Christmas season.

❖

232

Teach him to jump rope like a boxer.

❖

233

Help him make and send get-well cards to friends or relatives who are ill.

234
Take him to visit your state legislature
when it is in session.

❖

235
Make an appointment
to meet your Representative or Senator.

236
Visit a newspaper office
so he can see how the paper is produced.

❖

237
Let him have the money from cans he recycles.

❖

238
Limit what he watches on television
and how long he watches.

239
Listen to a baseball game on the radio
while doing other projects.

❖

240
Help him set up a roadside lemonade stand.

❖

241
Tell him who you voted for and why.

242

Give him a calendar
and help him fill in the birthdays
of family and friends.

243

Teach him the proper way
to answer the telephone
and how to respond to people's questions
over the phone.

244
Teach him that it is easier to lose trust
than to earn it.

❖

245
Compliment him
when he acts like a gentleman.

❖

246
Help him prepare a budget.

247
Start a matching savings plan for him.
Match every dollar
he puts into long-term savings.

248
Give him $10,000 of imaginary money.
Let him "invest" it in the stock market.
Together, see if he makes or loses money.

249
Teach him a new word each week.

❖

250
Help coach his baseball team.

❖

251
Write birthday messages on the car
with shoe polish.

252

Help your son make a list
of the ten people he admires the most,
and talk about the positive qualities
in their lives.

253

Make a list of what you will do
with all the money
if you win the ten-million-dollar sweepstakes.

254
Take him to an amusement park.

❖

255
Help him make a slingshot
out of a tree branch and oversized rubber bands.
Teach him to use his slingshot wisely.

❖

256
Go with him on a demonstration lesson
in a private plane.

257
Have a funeral when a pet dies.

❖

258
Get a new pet from the humane society.

❖

259
Watch television together.
Talk about the subtle messages of the program.

260
Let him talk first
when you call his grandparents.

❖

261
Make him eat good food,
but don't make him clean his plate.

❖

262
Always say positive things about his teachers.

263
Model and expect good table manners.

264
If you drive over the speed limit
or race through yellow lights,
don't expect him
to obey the rules you set for him.

265
Make a boat together.

❖

266
Get a children's book about a foreign language.
Work on learning it together.

❖

267
Go to father-son events and on outings.

268

Stop for ice cream on the way home.

❖

269

Take him with you when you play golf.

❖

270

Buy him his own fishing pole.

271

If he is on foot,
make sure he knows he is to be home
by the time the street lights come on.

❖

272

Look at *National Geographic* together.

❖

273

Don't make him eat liver.

274
Make friends
with those who coach his ball teams.

❖

275
Make sure he has a good pair of athletic shoes.

❖

276
Encourage him to save his own money
if he wants a better pair of athletic shoes.

277

Let him use your tools.

❖

278

Be sure he wears goggles
when he uses your tools.

❖

279

Be sure he puts your tools away after he uses them.

280
Buy him a weight-lifting set
that is appropriate to his strength.

❖

281
Put up an adjustable height basketball goal
in your driveway.

❖

282
Take a picture of him with a toothless grin.

283
Go with him to a toy or hobby store.
Watch which things he is attracted to.

❖

284
Get him a chemistry set.

❖

285
Give him a small trophy
when he achieves an important goal.

286
Take him to a professional rodeo
and get up close
to see the cowboys and stock
in action.

287
Encourage him to admire professional athletes
who are worthy of his admiration
on *and* off the field.

288

Take him to the park
and pitch him batting practice.

❖

289

Let him pick the restaurant
next time the family goes out.

❖

290

Get him an insulated sleeping bag.

291
Get a reading light for his bed.

❖

292
Do not allow him to pick on other children—
even siblings.

❖

293
Get him his own alarm clock.

294
Learn together
which generals fought in which wars.

❖

295
Design your dream house.

❖

296
Help him wash the dishes
when it isn't his turn.

297
Read the sports page together.

❖

298
Watch the evening news together
and discuss current events regularly.

❖

299
Volunteer to serve on parent-teacher committees
at his school.

300

Look for arrowheads in open areas
near your home.

❖

301

Take him to a public area known to have fossils.
Look for and gather them together.

❖

302

Take him canoeing on a scenic river.

303
Cook (and eat) foil dinners together
around a campfire.

❖

304
Make paper airplanes together
and see whose flies the farthest.

❖

305
Attend a hunters safety course together.

306
Take him to the top of the tallest building
near your home and view the surrounding area.
Try to find your house, his school,
and any other prominent landmarks.

❖

307
Give him one of your favorite hats
or T-shirts to keep and wear.

308
Take him to a fishing tackle store
and let him browse and browse.

309
Write to the President
and ask him for a photo of himself.
You will receive a picture
and a packet of information.

310
Have notepads printed with his name.

❖

311
Ask your state government
for the flag that was flown over the capital building
on your son's birthday.
(Many states provide
a limited number of free flags.)

312
Make and use tin can telephones.

313
Let him beat you in a race.

314
Place a bulletin board in his room
to display his artwork, photographs,
and certificates.

315
Play football together in the rain.

❖

316
Build a house of cards together.

❖

317
Run through the sprinklers together
on a hot summer day.

318
Buy him a compass.

❖

319
Buy him a magnet.

❖

320
Show him how a magnet affects a compass.

321

Have a picture of you and your son
enlarged to poster size.
Give it to him on a special occasion.

❖

322

Work on an art project together.

❖

323

Work on a science project together.

324
Don't make him eat things you won't eat.

325
Give him an afternoon
when you will do whatever he wishes.

326
Look at a set of blueprints together.
Explain the building process to him.

327
Designate a place in your home
to mark and measure your son's growth.

❖

328
On his birthday,
spend the day finding out
how many free meals, desserts,
and other birthday freebies
you can acquire from local restaurants
and businesses.

329
Buy a short section of rain gutter
and build a giant banana split in it together.
Invite his friends to eat it with him.

❖

330
Give him a mug or glass
with his name painted or imprinted on it.

331
Teach him about time zones
in different parts of the country.

❖

332
Help him learn to dress appropriately
for various occasions.

❖

333
Send him a package by overnight air delivery.

334

Look at an encyclopedia together.
Review what may be old information to you,
and learn along with him.

❖

335

Surprise him by having a name plate made
for his door.

336
Give him the opportunity to join scouting
or some other all boys activity.

❖

337
Always buy the candy, wrapping paper, light bulbs,
and fertilizer he sells in fund-raisers.

❖

338
Tell him he is running faster.

339
Take him and his best friend roller skating.

❖

340
Cook dinner for the family together
and clean up afterward.
Be sure Mom gets the night off.

❖

341
Let him see you reading.

342

Keep a special folder for his report cards,
so that he can have a record of his grades
through all of his school years.

343

Rent a video of a movie (or television series)
that you enjoyed as a boy
and watch it together.

344
Teach him how to throw a frisbee.
Practice together often.

345
Give him his own watch.

346
Let him select his notebook
and school supplies.

347
Check out a book from the library
so he can learn to identify trees in your region.

❖

348
Send him postcards when you are out of town.

❖

349
Tell him stories about growing up
with your siblings.

350
Take him with you
to listen to a political debate.

❖

351
Never tell him "Boys don't cry."

❖

352
Buy him cowboy boots.

353
Let him see how much you pay
for the monthly utilities bill.

❖

354
Put his school's bumper sticker on your car.

❖

355
Teach him riddles or jokes he can tell his friends.

356
Explain to him
why you choose to attend religious services,
or why you do not.

357
From the library
get a book about the history
of your city or county.

358
Encourage him to participate
in a wide variety of activities.

❖

359
Make your own code
with numbers representing letters.
Send each other coded messages.

360
Give up something for him
(golf, television, smoking, etc.).
He may not even know about it,
but it will remind you of his importance to you.

❖

361
Ask him to help you
change the oil in your car.

362

Let him use your binoculars.

❖

363

Visit a national park near your home.

❖

364

Answer his questions.

365
Tell him "I love you!"
as often as he can stand it.

❖

A FATHER'S NOTE:

"Helping your son climb the mountain of life to true manhood"

❖

In a world where we sense something is wrong with the way we live, we look to the captain at the helm of the ship in a stormy sea to steer us home safely. As you consider yourself as the captain of your family's ship and, moreover, your son's future in this world, I (Ken) hope you will give quality time to prepare your son for his voyage into manhood. It starts now, not when he is sixteen and driving or when he packs the car to go off to college. A lifetime of little building blocks will give him a firm foundation on which to stand.

Don't underestimate the power of tradition, whether it is a family event or a Saturday trip to the doughnut shop. These little events will provide a special bond of strength and character.

Be a student of your child, know him, not for who you want

him to be, but as one God has uniquely gifted and molded. Cheer him on and help him discover his passion and mission in life.

Surround your son with other strong men of integrity and sensitivity. This will provide an informal level of mentoring.

Two men, Dan Bolin and Sam Moreton, have been this to my two sons, Ragan and Spencer. Dan and Sam possess certain qualities of which I am void. For instance, Sam is an avid hunter, and he often took Ragan and Spencer with him. Dan, on the other hand, has a great ability to perform and gives people pleasure with his humor. Ragan and Spencer emulate these qualities in their own lives—qualities I could not have provided.

As a father, I am grateful for these relationships for Ragan and Spencer. Mentoring is a critical step in a young man's development of true manhood. Mentoring accomplishes this because it ties weakness, strength, dreams, and relationships together that will influence the next generation of leadership.

Finally, consider "fathers and the blessing." Don't let your son leave home without your blessing. This action is a statement of your strong commitment to your son and his future as a man. Reach out to your son with meaningful touch, spoken affirmation of love, respect, and acceptance. Write a letter to your son addressing all of these. This letter will become one of your son's most treasured possessions—something he can look back to in times of need and find comfort, knowing he has his "father's blessing."

Congratulations! You are now poised to help your son take another step in the steep climb up the mountain of life to true manhood. In these defining moments, take time to play, laugh, and enjoy your son today . . . for he will be gone tomorrow.

To contact the authors, please feel free to call or write:

Dan Bolin, President
Encouragement FM
P.O. Box 8525
Tyler, TX 75711
903-593-5863
dbolin@tyler.net

Ken Sutterfield, Executive Director
4 Ozark Mountain Road
Solgohachia, AR 72156-9552
ken@ozarkconference.org
1-800-935-camp

Fun ideas to show your daughter you care.

Written by the author of *How to Be Your Little Man's Dad*,
this book is filled with fun and practical ideas
to show your daughter how much you love her.

How to Be Your Daughter's Daddy (Dan Bolin)

Virtues and values never go out of style.

Originally published in the 1800s, these books give readers a glimpse of
what it was like to grow up one hundred years ago. Each short essay
addresses a different virtue or value and includes questions
to help spark thought and discussion.

Talks to Boys (Eleanor A. Hunter)
Talks to Girls (Eleanor A. Hunter)

To get your copies visit your local bookstore, call 1-800-366-7788
or log on to www.navpress.com. Ask for a FREE catalog of
NavPress Products. Offer **#BPA**.

NAVPRESS
BRINGING TRUTH TO LIFE
www.navpress.com